TOMMY TOOTLEY'S FART-ASTIC FAMILY: THE COMPLETE COLLECTION!

2025 Ran Cohen (Ranco). All rights reserved.
First printing edition: 2025
ISBN: 978-965-93184-5-2
Written by: Ran Cohen (Ranco)
Illustrated By: Daniel Egharevba

No part of this book may be reproduced, distributed, or transmitted in any form or by any means, including photocopying, recording, or other electronic or mechanical methods, without the prior written permission of the author, except in the case of brief quotations embodied in critical reviews and certain other noncommercial uses permitted by copyright law.

This book is a work of fiction. Names, characters, places, and incidents are products of the author's imagination or used fictitiously. Any resemblance to actual events, locales, or persons, living or dead, is purely coincidental.

Published by: Whale Tale Publishing

All inquiries should be directed to ranco@tommytootley.com

 www.tommytootley.com

Follow us: @TommyTootley

TOMMY TOOTLEY'S FART-ASTIC FAMILY

Welcome to the Wacky World of Tommy Tootley!

You're holding the ultimate Tootley adventure! This book brings together **all five** hilarious stories from the *Tommy Tootley's Fart-astic Family series* in one **big, smelly, and side-splitting collection**.

From road trips gone wrong to beachside blunders, and even a wild journey into the belly of a whale, every Tootley tale is packed with laughs, surprises, and plenty of toots!

Want Even More Fart-astic Fun?

6 Interactive Book Apps – Packed with Games & Giggles!
Available on the **Play Store** & **App Store** – tap, listen, and play!

- *Fart-astic Road Trip* FREE!
- *Winter Cabin Adventure*
- *Farts and Fun with Tootley*
- *A Day at the Beach*
- *Discovering Leviatopia*
- **and** the *Fart-astic Collection* - a 4-in-1 bundle

Each app features:
✓ **Interactive storybooks** – tap to hear sounds and bring the story to life
✓ **Coloring games** – create your own Tootley masterpiece
✓ **Jigsaw puzzles** – piece together the funniest Tootley moments
✓ **Memory games** – match the Tootley family and friends in silly poses, costumes, and fart-filled fun!

🔍 **Search for "Tommy Tootley" on the App Store or Play Store!**
📱 *Best enjoyed on a tablet or iPad for the full experience!*

Love to Color? Get the Tootley Coloring Books!
Available on **Amazon**, these books bring the smelly fun to life with pages you can color:
✏️ *The Tootley's Fart-astic Coloring Book – Volume 1*
✏️ *The Tootley's Fart-astic Coloring Book – Volume 2*
✏️ *The Tootley's Fart-astic Coloring Book – Character Edition*
   (50 Funny Poses to Color from the Tootley Family & Friends!)

Now, grab your book, get comfy, and prepare for a fart-astic ride with the Tootley family!

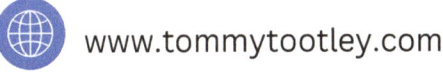 www.tommytootley.com   Follow us: @TommyTootley

Meet Mommy and Daddy Tootley!

Hi, I'm *Jenny Tootley*. I'm a high school teacher, but the real madness happens at home. I try to keep things clean and quiet... it never works. Daddy, *Tommy Tootley* is the biggest kid in the house. He's proud of his burps, his belly, and his brilliant bad ideas. He's always grumpy.
If something smells weird - it's usually him...

Jenny and Alex

Hi, I'm *Jenny*! I'm loud, bendy, and full of mischief. I can prank, fart, and giggle all at once - it's a talent. My brother *Alex* thinks he's the king of chaos. He's loud, messy, and laughs at his own toots. We're the best team - especially when we're causing trouble!

Luna

Woof. I'm *Luna*. I'm adorable.

I like snacks, naps, and peace.

The Tootleys? Loud. Gassy. Unpredictable.

Yesterday I dodged a fart and a flip-flop.

Today, I'm hiding under the couch. Wish me luck!

We Are the Tootley Family!

We're noisy, messy, stinky, and silly.

We love jokes, pranks, and each other (most of the time).

Every day is an adventure full of laughs and smells.

This is our family - and this is our story!

Hold your nose and come along!

The Great Adventure Begins

The Tootleys packed up for a winding ride,
To a stinky old cabin, where critters reside.
With Daddy and Mommy and two kids in tow,
And Luna the dog – will they make it? Who knows?

Snacks fill the car, the gas tank is full,
Burps and farts in the air, it's bound to be cool.
With laughs and surprises, they're ready to roam,
Will they reach the woods, or just turn back home?

Jenny's Snack-Splosion

Jenny gobbled snacks – cookies and cheese,
Munching and crunching, "More, please, please, please!"
But then her tummy gave a big, loud gurgle,
And up came the snacks in a messy swirl!

The car was filled with a yucky smell,
Mom, Dad, and Luna all yelled, "Oh well!"
"Quick, roll down the windows!" they said with dread,
While Jenny groaned and held down her head.

The Bottle Dilemma

"Please, Dad, can we stop? I really need to go!"
Alex was desperate; his discomfort started to show.
But Daddy kept driving, no place to be found,
So Alex grabbed a bottle and aimed to the ground.

He aimed, and he peed, Jenny burst out in cheer,
While Luna sat smiling, her joy crystal clear.
The family giggled at the silly little scene,
"Next time," said Mommy, "let's find a latrine!"

Are We There Yet?

"When will we get there?" Alex asked with a frown,
"Are we there yet, Daddy? Are we closer to town?"
Every five minutes, they'd ask once again,
Even though the GPS said hours remain!

Daddy just sighed, his patience so thin,
"Enough with the questions… Just look at the screen!"
But no matter the answer, they asked with delight,
"Are we there yet, Daddy? Is it still far in sight?"

A Toilet Catastrophe

Mommy needed to poop, no time to delay,
Daddy found a gas station, it was dirty and gray.
She rushed to the restroom, holding her breath,
The smelliest place on all planet Earth!

But as she stood up, her phone took a dive,
Right into the toilet – it didn't survive!
She flushed in a panic and cried out in dismay,
"My phone's gone for good – this just ruined my day!"

The Burger Blunder

The Tootleys sat down, ready to munch,
Ordered big burgers, their favorite lunch.
But once on the road, their bellies went wild,
Jenny felt sick, no longer smiled.

Alex let out a fart, wet and loud,
Luna hid her face, away from the crowd.
The whole car stunk, it was gross and mad,
They all groaned together, "Those burgers were bad!"

The Tootley Tummy Trouble

Lunch was awful, then things got worse,
The car was filled with a stinky burst!
Alex and Luna let out some gas,
Daddy's loud burps just wouldn't pass!

Mommy was yawning, her eyes half closed,
Then Alex threw up – Mommy froze!
The whole car smelled like a giant shoe,
"Oh no!" they all cried, "What did we do?"

Wake Up, Daddy!

Seven hours in, Daddy's eyes grow tight,
His eyelids droop, losing his sight.
Mommy sprays him with water, right to his face,
"Stay awake, Daddy, keep up the pace!"

But Daddy still dozes, slipping into sleep,
Luna starts barking, loud and deep.
Mommy slaps Daddy, to wake him with care,
Daddy's back to driving, alert and aware.

The Wrong Way Adventure

Daddy missed a sign, took the wrong track,
The road was all snowy, no way to turn back.
"Recalculating route!" the GPS shout,
But the Tootleys were lost, there was no way out!

Alex made ghost sounds, "Oooooo, beware!"
Jenny whispered, "Stop it, I'm scared!"
Mommy was nervous, "Are we really lost?"
Daddy just replied, "Oh, we'll get across!"

The Bathroom Line Disaster

They found a rest stop, but the line was a crawl,
Alex and Jenny felt the urgent call.
They danced and they shuffled, trying to stay cool,
But the wait dragged on, making them drool!

When they finally got in, no paper in sight!
Mommy and Daddy laughed, "Oh, what a night!"
Jenny sighed and Alex groaned, desperate to find,
So they used the map, to wipe their behind.

The Cold Cabin Quest

The Tootleys arrived at their cabin so old,
Snow on the ground, silent and cold.
A week full of plans, for family and fun,
Cooking and hiking, in the frosty sun.

Will they all bond, with a laughter and cheer?
Or will they wish to be far, far from here?
With snowflakes and cocoa, they'll try their best,
Will they make it through this freezing test?

The Cabin Chaos

After ten long hours, they reached the gate,
But where's the key? They searched and they wait.
When they found it at last, they opened the door,
Rushing inside, their feet were so sore.

They ran to the toilet and then to the shower,
But no water, no light, not even power!
The cabin was freezing, like a giant ice block,
"No water, no lights – what a cold, hard shock!"

Mom to the Rescue

The pipes were frozen, no water would flow,
The lights all went out, as the wires did blow.
Daddy tried fixing, with tape and some glue,
But nothing worked, what would they do?

Mommy stepped in, with a confident grin,
She twisted and turned, and plugged it right in.
With just a few clicks, the lights came back bright,
Daddy blushed, "Guess you're always right!"

Luna the Peacemaker

Alex dashed in, "The big room is mine!"
But Jenny got there first, in record time.
Alex was yelling, Jenny in tears,
Luna came running, calming their fears.

She wiggled between them, wagging her tail,
They both started petting, forgetting to wail.
Luna's the hero, she made things right,
Now everyone's happy, ready for night!

The Fireplace Fumble

Daddy brought logs from the pile out back,
He missed the big plastic stuck in the stack.
He tossed it inside, the fire did roar,
But smoke filled the cabin, from ceiling to floor!

Luna barked loudly, they all had to flee,
Running outside, to air that was free.
Coughing and gasping, they stood in the snow,
"Next time," said Mommy, "check what you throw!"

The Fart-astic Feast

They gathered for dinner, by the fire so bright,
Beans, broccoli, and soda – a true delight!
They ate up their food, not knowing the cost,
Soon farts filled the cabin, they laughed and got tossed!

The smell was so strong, it made Luna roar,
Jenny asked, "Will our farts freeze by the door?"
Mommy just chuckled, "They might in cold air,
If you let them outside – see if you dare!"

Luna's Snowy Rescue

The family set out for an evening walk,
Through snow-covered trees, and a cozy talk.
But after an hour, they were all turned around,
Lost in the snow, with no way to be found.

Luna took charge, her nose to the ground,
She sniffed out the path, without making a sound.
She led them back safely, through snow soft and deep,
They gave her big hugs, then drifted to sleep!

The Stinky Chimney Caper

Daddy decided to clean the chimney tall,
He climbed up the roof, afraid he might fall.
But as he swept down, soot covered his face,
He sneezed out a cloud all over the place!

With black smoke and sneezes, the air smelled so bad,
The Tootleys all laughed, "Poor sooty Dad!"
He climbed down and sniffled, covered in grime,
Then let out a burp – it was truly slime!

The Smelly Hide and Seek

They played hide and seek inside the small space,
Daddy squeezed in a cupboard – what a funny place!
He tried not to giggle, he tried not to peek,
But he felt something coming, a small, sneaky squeak!

With a big, loud fart, his spot was revealed,
The kids heard the noise and giggled, then squealed.
They opened the door and pulled him out fast,
"Stuck in that stench, you could've choked on the blast!"

The Bone Bandit

The Tootleys woke up, to a morning of white,
They ran out to build a snowman with delight.
They found some old bones, and thought it was fun,
To use them as limbs, sticking out one by one.

But Luna saw bones, and couldn't resist,
She jumped at the snowman, no detail was missed!
She tore it apart, with the bones in her jaw,
She jumped all around, as they watched in awe!

Wordplay on Wheels

We're all in the car
With Jenny's friend, Buzz,
Playing with words,
As a smart family does.
"Combine 'breakfast' and 'lunch'" Mom says as she grins,
"Brunch!" we shout, and the fun begins.
"Now, 'smoke' and 'fog' – what word do you get?"
"Smog!" we cheer, not breaking a sweat.
And Buzz whispers shyly, with a bit of unease,
"In your car, these words – you mix with such ease,
But in ours?
We just fart, laugh, and do as we please..."

The Burp that Shook the House

In the living room, Daddy's at play,
On his phone, a silly little game.
Suddenly, he burps, with a sound so strong,
Making Mom jump, saying, "Yikes, what's wrong?"

"What's that noise – that terrible sound?
Did something break or crash to the ground?"
No, it's just Daddy, caught by surprise,
His burp made him lose, now he's rolling his eyes!

The Farting Game

Playing with a friend under the sheet,
The rule is simple – no retreat.
Each takes a turn with a toot so loud,
Then we breathe in – no escaping allowed!

The last one to stay wins the game,
And proudly basks in their claim to fame,
For if you can endure the stinky air,
You're the master of the breeze, beyond compare!

Mom's Mighty Sneeze

Mom dusts off some books,
As dust tickles her nose.
She rears back to sneeze,
And out comes a blast – it blows!

Daddy faints on the spot,
The dog dives under a chair.
My Brother yawns and says: "Bless you,"
And keeps humming without a care.

The Mystery Stench

Sitting in the living room, we're caught by surprise.
By a sudden stench, as if something had died.
We glanced at each other, with questioning eyes.
Wondering who had something to hide.

Each one of us claimed, "No! it wasn't me!"
With innocent grins, as clear as could be.
And under the table, the dog laying low,
Wagging her tail – "ah, the culprit we know".

The Morning Crisis

Getting ready for preschool, we're running a bit late,
The house is rumbling in a chaotic state.
My sister is crying, her eyes full of fear,
"I have to poop – mom, so please wait here!"

"Then what's the hold-up? Just go, don't stall,"
Says Mom, with a voice that's not at all small.
"But it's just not possible, Dad was just there,
And the smell that he left is too much to bear!"

Who was it?!

Who was that? I heard a fart?
Mom, Dad, Sis – who's playing smart?
No way, no one's to blame?
Come on, own up – name the name!

Maybe it's the dog, with her innocent face,
Truly asleep in her usual place.
Dreaming of fields on a moonlit night,
And now, right here, she's let one take flight...

The Trumpet Blast

"Who's playing music at noon?"
Mother asked.
"I think I heard a trumpet blast!"

"Oh, it's just Dad blowing his nose,"
my brother said.
"It tickled him terribly – now his nose is red!"

Mega Loogie Launch

The grossest thing in the world, no doubt,
Is riding with Dad when we're out and about.
When suddenly he opens the window wide,
And does something that makes me want to hide.

He sniffs hard, clearing his throat with might,
Then spits out the window, something slimy and bright -
A giant, green glob that flies with such ease,
It's so disgusting, I wish I could unsee that, please!

The Sweaty Classroom

Mom came home from school,
With tears welled in her eyes.
She'd taught right after gym class –
The smell could paralyze!

Her students dripped from head to toe,
The stench was off the chart.
"Why must sweat smell so awful?"
She sighed with all her heart.

Ready for the Beach

The sun was shining, the sky so clear,
The Tootleys packed up all their beach gear.
Sunscreen, shades, and surfboards bright,
A giant sea mattress, a boat packed tight!

With hats on heads and bags by their side,
They hopped in the car, all ready to ride.
"Looks like we've got it all!" Daddy said with pride,
As the adventure began, and fun waited outside!

The Gusty Beach Adventure

They reached the beach, found the perfect spot,
Unpacked their things, the sun was hot.
Daddy built the tent, sturdy and strong,
While the kids grabbed their boards to catch waves all day long.
But a strong gust came, and in seconds it blew,
Mommy's hat and the tent went flying, too!
Daddy groaned, "Not again!" as he ran to retrieve,
But the Tootleys just laughed – what a day to believe!

Golden Surprise!

Jenny dug fast, with a laugh and a cheer,
Daddy lay buried, sand up to his ear.
Only his head poked out in the sun,
They both laughed – this was so much fun!

But here came Luna, her tail wagging wide,
She sniffed at the sand and sat by his side.
And before he could shout or scramble to flee,
She lifted her leg and let out a pee!

Snapped on the Snout

Luna played by the shore, splashing around,
She pounced on a rock she thought she had found.
But the rock gave a snap and grabbed her nose tight –
It wasn't a rock, but a crab with a bite!

She yelped and she ran, with a crab on her face,
The Tootleys all laughed at the wild chase.
Round and around, poor Luna sped,
A crab clinging tight to the top of her head!

The Sandcastle Washout

The kids built a castle, tall and grand,
Close to the shore, right there on the sand.
They smiled with pride, "It's ready to stay!"
But the tide rushed in and washed it away.

Luna sat by, her tail drooping low,
Watching the waves take it with the flow.
She whimpered and whined, her eyes full of gloom,
As the castle sank into the water's tomb.

The Farting Contest

The Tootleys jumped in, splashing away,
"Let's have a contest!" Jenny did say.
"Whose fart will be heard from under the waves?"
They giggled and bubbled, as brave as the braves.

Alex let one rip, it startled a fish,
Then bumped a jelly with a watery swish!
The jellyfish shot up, causing a big splash,
And Alex won the contest with a fart so brash!

Fishy Frenzy

The Tootleys relaxed, floating with ease,
Enjoying the waves and the warm summer breeze.
But suddenly fishes began to bite,
Nibbling their legs, sparking some fright!

They screamed and they ran, straight to the shore,
But stepped on sharp pebbles that made them all roar!
Hopping and yelping, they jumped in surprise,
"Next time," said Daddy, "Shoes would be wise!"

Beach Bat Fetch

Daddy and Mommy were having a blast,
Playing with beach bats, the ball flying fast.
But when it went far, who saved the day?
Luna, the ball dog, rushed into play!

She dashed through the sand, her tail wagging wide,
Fetching the ball with joy and with pride.
Back to the game, she'd run with delight,
Luna, the hero, made everything right!

The Sneeze Set Sail

The family lounged on their sea mattress wide,
Floating along on a calm, gentle ride.
But then Daddy sneezed, so loud and strong,
And suddenly, they were zooming along!

They sped through the waves, far out of sight,
Towards a whale-shaped island, oh what a fright!
The Tootleys held on as they sailed with a cheer,
An adventure ahead, and the island was near!

Whale of a Surprise

As they neared the island, the water spun round,
A gentle whirlpool pulled them down.
It carried them softly, without a scare,
To a place so strange, but full of air.

They landed inside a whale, soft and wide,
With streets and lights glowing deep inside.
"Welcome to Leviatopia!" the Tootleys were told,
A magical city where adventures unfold!

Discovering Leviatopia!

It started at the beach, with sand and sun,
The Tootleys were having a day of fun.
Squeezed on a mattress, floating with ease,
When suddenly – Daddy let out a sneeze!

They flew so fast, it felt like a sail,
Toward an island with quite the tale.
A whirlpool spun, they all turned pale,
When they found themselves inside a whale!

Hello to you!

My name is Levi the whale,
and I'm happy to have you as guests in my city!

I apologize for speaking through this
communication system, but I have no choice.
You see - you are in and I am out!

Welcome to my city - Leviatopia,
The place that's perfect for all,
Where anything you want is yours,
And you're certain to have a ball.
Welcome to Leviatopia,
The best place on all planet Earth,
Where you can do anything at all,
And it's free, no matter its worth!

Meeting Levi the Whale

The Tootleys stared, and Jenny whispered – "mommy,
A talking whale with a city in its tummy?"
Buildings and roads, all inside,
A magical world, so vast and wide.

People were walking, streets wound around,
Shocked and amazed, they made not a sound.
A whole hidden city, so grand to see,
The Tootleys just gaped, as amazed as could be.

Carry on straight down the mall,

All covered in jewels and gold.

Then, stop at the gigantic arch.

Go on now, before I grow old!

The Amusement Park Adventure

Levy led them to the park, through an arch so wide,
"This ride is the best!" Levy pointed with pride.
The Tootleys climbed in, packed in nice and tight.
Ready for laughter, thrills, and delight.

Up they soared, then twisted around,
Mom shrieked loudly, Dad fainted mid-round.
Alex turned green, his stomach upset,
While Jenny just giggled – "the best ride yet!!"

Want to see my flying zoo?!
Wondrous, magical things happen
In my city called Leviatopia.
Anything is possible here,
Because my city is a utopia!

You can play and dance and walk and swim,
Live each dream and indulge every whim.
You can even fly here, if you wish,
Just choose any animal, even a fish.

The Flying Zoo Fiasco

The Tootleys walked in, amazed by the view,
Jenny grabbed a zebra's tail – what else could she do?
The zebra took off, flying fast, wild as can be,
Jenny held on tight, laughing with glee!

Alex found an elephant, floating up high,
He held on tight as it soared through the sky!
Daddy got pecked by an ostrich on ground,
He ran in circles, yelling loud all around!

Just past the park there's a super place

If hunger is what you feel.

All your favorites will be there.

Today's special? A tasty Kid's Meal!

The Super Feast

The Tootleys walked in, eyes open so wide,
A restaurant filled with food on every side!
They started to order, dish after dish,
Mountains of burgers, fries, and some fish.

The kids asked for toys that came with each meal,
All the shiny treasures made them squeal!
They feasted like pigs, till they thought they'd explode,
Dad felt like puking, Mom ran to unload!

Do you want to continue?

At the avenue's end climb five stairs,
Then head down the road for a treat.
Turn into the lane, and you'll understand
Why I think you're both so sweet.

The Enormous Candy Shop

The Tootleys stepped in, their jaws dropped in awe,
Candy stacked high on every shelf they saw!
Jenny grabbed gummies, pulled more than her share,
While Alex picked candies with toys everywhere.

Jenny got gum stuck all over her hair,
And Luna licked chocolate – oops, beware!
She started to gag, her tummy felt bad,
Mom looked worried, and Dad was quite mad.

If you want to have some fun,

Around the corner you will find,

A special fountain just for you,

With sparkling waters and magic too!

The Magical Fountain

The Tootleys approached, excited to see,
What magic and fun at the fountain would be.
Daddy drank a sip, and bubbles came out,
Floating from his mouth, laughing out loud!

Jenny jumped in and started to float in the air,
Popping his bubbles with laughter and flair.
Then Luna jumped in, making everyone cheer,
Water splashed out of her nose and her ears!

The Food Truck Snack

The Tootleys were hungry, craving a bite,
They spotted a food truck, just before night.
Daddy grabbed a snack that was bubbly and sweet,
And hiccupped big bubbles with every bite he'd eat!

Alex chose a candy called 'Fart-tastic Treat',
He started to toot they all wanted to flee!
The family laughed, the whole park roared,
As bubbles and toots made sure none were bored!

You still have time for one more thrill.
Turn here to the left, and you'll see a hill.
Climb right to the top, and there on the peak
You'll find the elevator that you seek.

Press the button marked 'Minus 4',
And you'll find a place that you'll adore.
Deep in the hill is hidden a store
With everything you wish for and more!

The Purple Dwarf

The Tootleys arrived at the biggest store,
A purple dwarf greeted them right by the door.
"Welcome inside, come see the surprise,
Enjoy yourselves, pick anything you like!"

The Magical Toy Store Adventure

The shelves were filled with toys of all kinds,
Teddies and trucks, things that wind.
The kids were in shock, their eyes open wide,
The parents were worried, but couldn't hide.

Jenny grabbed dolls, Alex found a plane,
Mom shook her head, it all seemed insane.
The dwarf just giggled, his grin full of glee,
"Take what you like, it's all truly free!"

Should you wish to visit again,
In the place where we met, please stand.
Then just call out the secret password,
Together hand in hand.

Just call out 'Levi! Levi!'
Then call out 'Levi' once more.
If it's important, be patient,
And I'll come, even from afar!

Goodbye, Levi!

The Tootleys said, "Thanks, Levi, now help us get back!"
Levi smiled and said, "I've got just the knack"
He placed them back on the mattress he'd stored,
Then gave a huge push with his tail like a board.

They sailed so fast, like a speedboat ride,
Through waves and foam, with laughter and pride.
Back to the shore where they had begun,
The Tootleys arrived, their adventure now done.

THE END

Thank you for laughing, tooting,
and tagging along -
the Tootleys will be back with more!

We hope you enjoyed the Wacky World of Tommy Tootley!

Want Even More Fart-astic Fun?
6 Interactive Book Apps – Packed with Games & Giggles!
Available on the **Play Store** & **App Store** – tap, listen, and play!

- Fart-astic Road Trip *FREE!*
- Winter Cabin Adventure
- Farts and Fun with Tootley
- A Day at the Beach
- Discovering Leviatopia
- and the Fart-astic Collection - a 4-in-1 bundle

Each app features:
✓ **Interactive storybooks** – tap to hear sounds and bring the story to life
✓ **Coloring games** – create your own Tootley masterpiece
✓ **Jigsaw puzzles** – piece together the funniest Tootley moments
✓ **Memory games** – match the Tootley family and friends in silly poses, costumes, and fart-filled fun!

🔍 Search for "*Tommy Tootley*" on the App Store or Play Store!
Best enjoyed on a tablet or iPad for the full experience!

Love to Color? Get the Tootley Coloring Books!
Available on **Amazon**, these books bring the smelly fun to life with pages you can color:
🖍 *The Tootley's Fart-astic Coloring Book – Volume 1*
🖍 *The Tootley's Fart-astic Coloring Book – Volume 2*
🖍 *The Tootley's Fart-astic Coloring Book – Character Edition*
   (50 Funny Poses to Color from the Tootley Family & Friends!)

   www.tommytootley.com   Follow us: @TommyTootley

www.ingramcontent.com/pod-product-compliance
Lightning Source LLC
LaVergne TN
LVHW070603070526
838199LV00011B/476